The Curtain Ca

DANCE PERFORMANCE

From Rehearsal to Opening Night

Kristin Kessel

The Rosen Publishing Group, Inc., New York

Special thanks to Maria DiDia

Published in 2004 by The Rosen Publishing Group, Inc.
29 East 21st Street, New York, NY 10010

First Edition

Library of Congress Cataloging-in-Publication Data

Kessel, Kristin.
    Dance performance : from rehearsal to opening night / by Kristin
    Kessel.—1st ed.
    p. cm.— (The curtain call library of dance)
    Summary: Explores what it takes to prepare for and participate in a
    dance performance from the point of view of a dancer.
    ISBN 0-8239-4556-1 (lib. bdg.)
    1. Dance—Juvenile literature. 2. Dancers—Juvenile literature. [1.
    Dance. 2. Dancers.] I. Title. II. Series.

    GV1596.5.K47 2004
    792.8—dc21

                                       2003012409

Manufactured in the United States of America

CONTENTS

INTRODUCTION

You arrive at the theater on opening night. There are bouquets of flowers everywhere. You sense excitement in the air as you warm up with the other dancers. You head to your dressing room to apply your stage makeup. As you carefully put on your costume, you go over the choreography in your mind for the last time.

"Places, everyone!" shouts the stage manager. You head backstage and take a few deep breaths. The music begins and the curtain rises. You feel the heat of the stage lights and the energy of the other dancers around you. You run onto the stage and dance as you've never danced before. When you hit your final pose, the audience roars! The sound of clapping rings in your ears.

You and the other dancers take your final bow and the curtain comes down. The performance was a huge success!

A lifetime of performing onstage can begin with a single dance recital. Learning and practicing choreography, and working with your dance classmates toward a performance is a wonderful experience. It is a chance to show an audience what you can do—and an opportunity to become comfortable as a performer.

Long before any performance, however, are hours of practicing and perfecting the show. The process is hard work—and lots of fun. So let's leap into the incredible world of dance performance—from rehearsal to opening night!

With enough practice, you will gain the confidence to completely throw yourself into your performance.

CHAPTER 1
THE REHEARSAL PROCESS

Every dancer remembers the first time he or she felt the magic of performing onstage. It is a thrilling experience, in which the body is used to communicate the theme, mood, and sometimes even the plot of a story to an audience. It is your chance, as a dancer, to share your talent with the world.

Many dancers first experience being onstage in their dance class recitals. In recitals, the members of a dance class perform for their friends and family. Recitals generally take place at the end of a year of dance classes. This gives the dancers an opportunity to show off what they have learned—and the chance to do it in the spotlight.

Before any performance, however, comes the rehearsal process. This process is a combination of fun, hard work, and dedication that leads to the best possible reward: dancing onstage!

Gotta Dance

Accomplished performer Jim Borstelmann of *Jerome Robbins' Broadway*, *Damn Yankees*, *Chicago*, and *The Producers* explains his passion for professional dancing. "I didn't choose this career, it chose me. I love to perform....Dance? Gotta do it. It's fun. It's what I was put on this Earth to do."

Practice Makes Perfect

Preparing for a recital is an exciting process. Since everyone in a dance class generally takes part in a recital, rehearsals are often part of the class. In regular dance class, you will learn, practice, and perfect dances. As the recital nears, you will begin to learn and perfect the choreography, or sequence of dance steps, you will perform onstage. Most

● The many hours you spend rehearsing will feel worth it once the spotlight shines on opening night.

likely, your teacher will act as the choreographer. This is the person who creates the dances and teaches them to you.

Your Job

Your job as a dancer is to give your teacher your full attention. In many cases you'll begin learning your recital choreography within the first few months of class and continue to expand it up to the weeks before the show. Many dancers find this system helpful because it gives them all year to perfect the steps they'll perform onstage.

As recital time approaches, your teacher may introduce new, more difficult steps to add to your class's choreography. Focus on your technique and try to improve your skills as you learn each one. Always try your best and remember to practice at home. Ask your teacher for assistance if you need help with a certain movement and ask your fellow dancers to review the steps with you.

Helpful Hints

Some dancers find it helpful to take notes on the choreography they learn. Dancers often come up with their own systems of symbols, words, and pictures to write down the order of steps. Recording the music played during class can also be useful. With the notes and music, you can practice at home.

● Pay close attention to your teacher as he or she introduces new steps to the class—you might end up performing them in front of an audience.

Dance Groupings

There are different types of dances that may be added to your choreography. A solo is a dance performed by only one dancer. A duet is a dance for two dancers, sometimes

● It is important to learn to share the stage with the dancers around you. Everyone must work together for a successful group performance.

called a pas de deux. A trio is for three, and a quartet, sometimes called a pas de quatre, is for four dancers. There are

● Timing is *everything* in a dance performance. It is more than simply doing the movements properly—you must perform each one at the perfect moment.

also dances for small groups, made up of five to twelve dancers. Larger group dances are called ensemble pieces.

Dancing with a group is a wonderful experience. Dance classes and recital rehearsals are a good place to make friends and learn from each other. During these rehearsals, you'll discover the importance of cooperation and teamwork as you bring the choreography to life. There is often "down time" during rehearsals when your teacher is working with another group of dancers and you have to wait for your turn. Be patient and practice with your fellow dancers. You can learn a lot from your classmates. Focus on working together. Remember, even a solo dance is not a solo performance. No divas allowed!

Cleaning It Up

After you have learned all of the choreography for your recital, you will begin a series of rehearsals called "cleaning up" ("cleanup" for short) or "touch-up" rehearsals. These rehearsals usually start about three weeks before the performance and are held during your regular class time. At these rehearsals, you will dance your choreography over and over again. If necessary, your teacher will make specific changes and corrections.

In your dance classes, you do most of your work in front of a mirror. For the recital, however, you'll have to build the confidence to dance without seeing your reflection. To prepare you for this, your teacher may ask you to practice with your back to the mirror or may even cover the mirror completely. While it might feel strange at first, dancing without relying on your reflection is the best way to prepare for dancing onstage.

During cleanup rehearsals, you will practice each section of the choreography until it is as close to perfect as it can be. A foot or a hand just an inch off of its proper placement can visually ruin a performance. Use these rehearsals as an opportunity to focus on your body and perfect your technique. Concentrate on carrying out each step gracefully.

● Dancing without watching your reflection can be difficult. However, it is an important part of moving from the classroom to the stage.

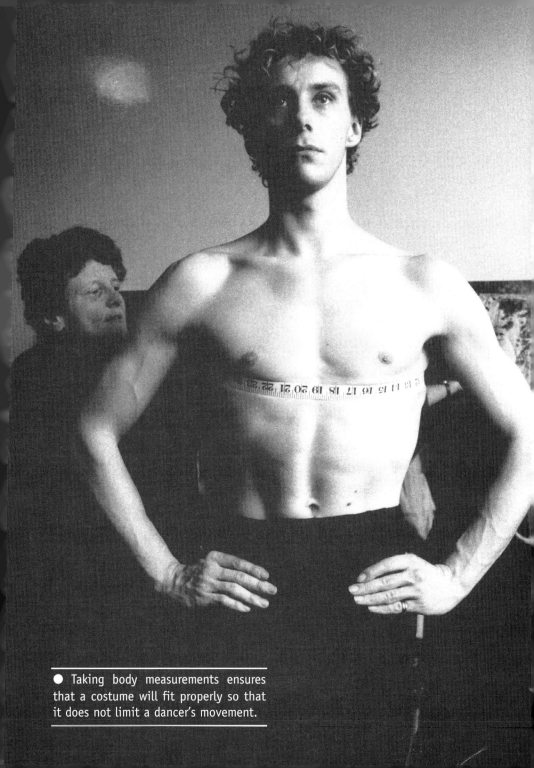

● Taking body measurements ensures that a costume will fit properly so that it does not limit a dancer's movement.

Cleanup rehearsals are an exciting part of the rehearsal process. They give you the opportunity to see how much your class has improved.

Getting Your Costume

A few months before the recital, your teacher will measure each dancer in class for a costume. These measurements are important because they ensure that your costume will fit correctly. Your teacher will choose costumes that reflect your dance's theme and choreography. If you're lucky, you may even get to see a picture of the costumes in a catalog.

The process of getting your costume is very exciting. You might be tempted to wear it before the show. Remember, however, the importance of keeping it clean and safe for the recital. It has to look fabulous onstage!

It is a good idea to find out how to care for your costume. Do not make any alterations unless you are given permission by your teacher. Make sure not to eat or drink in or around your costume, as it could get stained or ruined. Hang it in a safe place and it will be perfect for opening night.

Smile!

Some dance studios arrange for photographs to be taken of each dance class in their costumes. If your studio does so, you will take a group photo with your class and then some shots of you alone.

● Costumes that fit right and are taken care of help make you look terrific onstage.

You and your parents will then be able to purchase the pictures from the photographer as souvenirs from the performance.

15

CHAPTER 2
GOOD REHEARSAL HABITS

It takes a lot of dedicated people to put a show together. Each person must do his or her part to ensure the show will be a success. As a dancer, you will contribute by working hard toward a great performance—and having fun each step of the way!

Attendance

It is important to be present at every scheduled rehearsal. Each one is an opportunity for you to learn and participate, and is the next step toward a fabulous show. You are part of a team that can only succeed if each member contributes equally. If dancers are missing from rehearsals, how will the show improve before the recital?

Of course, emergencies come up. Limit your absences to unexpected illnesses or family obligations. Make sure to notify your teacher if you are going to miss a rehearsal. Then get together with another dancer to go over what you missed. This way, you will be caught up with the rest of the class at the next rehearsal.

Attentiveness

Every rehearsal is a chance for you to absorb more knowledge about dance. While you are there, be as alert and attentive as possible. Observe your teacher and watch how other dancers work together. If you are confused about

● Veteran performer Chita Rivera of *West Side Story*, *Chicago*, and many other shows, once explained her emotional connection to dancing. She said, "Dance is something inside me that needs to come out all the time."

something, ask for help. Save questions about the performance in general for after rehearsal. However, raising your hand to ask about a certain step is perfectly okay. Chances are you are not the only one who needs help. Communicating with your teacher and your fellow dancers will give them the chance to get to know you—and learning from others can help you grow as a performer.

Taking Care of Your Body

Preparing for a performance requires a lot of energy. You'll need to be ready to dance through long rehearsals. Eating a healthy, balanced diet will keep your energy level high. Make sure to eat a nourishing mix of foods, including fresh produce, whole grains, meats, fish, and dairy products. A sensible combination of protein, fat, and carbohydrates will keep you healthy and strong.

Most dancers do not like eating a large meal before a rehearsal or a performance. Being too full can cause you to feel heavy or tired while you move and might keep you from doing your best. Listen to your body and do what feels best for you. Keep healthy snacks like fruit, vegetables, or nuts handy for an energy boost.

Make sure that you are drinking enough water to stay hydrated. Your body loses a lot of water as you sweat. You'll need to replenish this water so you can dance properly. Keep a water bottle handy and be sure to take sips at appropriate times during class.

Fun Fact

Staying healthy isn't just about healthy eating. Your body also needs to rest. Try to get at least eight hours of sleep each night and sneak naps into your day if you can. This will keep you strong and rested—and give any sore muscles a chance to heal.

Balancing Act

Rehearsals and performances can take up a lot of your time. It is your responsibility to stay on top of your schoolwork. Staying organized will help you balance dancing with school, friends, and family. Many dancers find it helpful to create schedules to manage their time. With a schedule, you can set aside a certain amount of time each day for homework, so you'll stay on top of your studies. Inform your teachers about your rehearsals and ask for extra help if you need it. If you show them you are working hard to keep up, they will be more than willing to help you succeed.

Family and Friends

Find ways to include your friends and family in your dancing. Your teacher may even need them to volunteer to help out with the show. Including the important people in your life in the excitement of the show will help them understand that performing is important to you. They will see that your time and energy are focused on something very special.

● As your recital approaches, you will rehearse more frequently. Make sure you stay on top of your schoolwork even though you have less free time.

19

CHAPTER 3
MOVING TO THE THEATER

Your recital will take place somewhere that has a stage area and a place for an audience. It might be a school auditorium, yet you should think of it as a theater. You will always remember the first time you enter the place in which you first performed. The hustle and bustle of the

● Performing in a theater is a thrilling experience. Being onstage, under lights, and in front of an audience is a dream come true for many dancers.

backstage area, the stage itself, and even the smell of the theater come together to make the experience magical. As you look at the many rows of empty seats, picture them filled by an excited audience on opening night!

Getting Technical

When you move to the theater, all of the technical aspects of the show come together. This includes the sound and lighting, which are rehearsed and perfected. Sometimes these elements will come together at the dress rehearsal, just before the recital. In other cases, there are special technical rehearsals, or "tech" rehearsals for short.

During tech rehearsals, your teacher or choreographer will work with a lighting design-

● For a performance, dancers are lit from many angles to help create the mood for the dance.

er, sound designer, set designers, and a stage manager, as the dancers perform different parts of the show. Often parents of performing dancers volunteer for these important tech jobs. With their help, the show will run as smoothly as possible.

The teacher may ask the dancers to stop several times

as they rehearse. Each dance needs to be "spaced" on the stage. Spacing is an important part of the process in which dancers are spread out across the stage to create the best overall look. Your teacher may mark the stage with numbers so that each dancer knows where he or she should be. Often the teacher will have introduced these number marks on the floor of your dance studio before the rehearsals moved to the theater.

While this happens, the teacher also explains when specific changes in sound or lighting should take place. Different combinations of these changes will be tried to make the performance look and sound better. Once choices are made, each sound and lighting change is given a number called a cue. Cues activate the changes and mark important moments in the show. Both the dancers and the technical crew need to be aware of the cues to ensure the show is successful.

Dressing the Part

As the recital approaches, you will have a dress rehearsal. A dress rehearsal is a practice run of the entire performance.

Helpful Hint

Make sure that you confirm with your teacher how to secure closures and straps on your costumes with either safety pins or small stitches. A parent dresser can help you. It is also important to find proper undergarments to wear with your costume. You don't want the audience to see anything peeking out that shouldn't be!

Every aspect of the show finally comes together, just as they will in front of an audience. Each member of the

Proper stage makeup and a beautiful costume can help bring a dance to life.

cast and crew performs his or her job as if it were opening night.

For first-time performers, a dress rehearsal might be the first time you wear stage makeup. Bright stage lights can make performers look

pale or washed out. Dramatic stage makeup can prevent this. If you have never applied stage makeup, observe another dancer doing it or ask for help. Very often your teacher or a special makeup designer will advise the cast on what to do. Your teacher may also decide on a specific hairstyle for each class to go along with the makeup, costumes, and choreography. At dress rehearsal, you will have the opportunity to practice your hair and makeup as well as any quick costume changes that may have to be made during the performance.

Dressing Rooms

Dressing rooms are backstage spaces for performers in which they dress and prepare for a show. Usually, dancers share one large dressing space. Sharing a room can be a lot of fun. It presents a great opportunity to make friends, help each other out with costumes and makeup, and share the excitement of performing. Often, there will be parent volunteers in every dressing room to help out with costumes, makeup, and hair.

There are separate dressing rooms for male and female dancers. Many dancers like to decorate dressing rooms with posters and good luck charms for inspiration. In each room, there are mirrors surrounded by bright white lights. These lights imitate the brightness of stage lights, so performers can apply the appropriate amount of makeup.

Since many dancers will be sharing one space, it is important for everyone to show consideration for their fellow performers. Show respect for the other dancers, as well as the theater, by keeping your dressing space neat.

● Sharing a dressing space with other dancers is a lot of fun. You can make friends and learn helpful tips on makeup and costume care.

The Stage

As your teacher communicates to your class about the stage, he or she will use stage directions. If a performer is told to exit "stage right," the director is referring to the performer's right side as he or she faces the audience. "Stage left" refers to the stage on the performer's left as he or she

25

faces the audience. "Upstage" is the end of the stage, the part farthest away from the audience. "Downstage" is the front of the stage.

On the sides of the stage are areas called wings. The wings are used for storing scenery and lights. They are also where dancers enter and exit

● Remember to stay out of sight while waiting in the wings.

☆Opening Night Advice

Professional performer Bebe Neuwirth of *A Chorus Line*, *Dancin'*, *Sweet Charity*, *Damn Yankees*, *Chicago*, and *Fosse* offers the following advice to dancers: "Behave yourself. Be courteous. Be professional. Respect your fellow performers and the building—the theater."

Lights

Lighting is an important part of a performance. It helps set the mood of a show for the audience. For dance performances, lights are hung from a fly system, a series of poles and rails above the stage, as well as on poles placed around the stage and theater. The extent to which a dance performance is lit depends on the size of the theater and the budget for the show.

the stage. There are curtains, called teasers, in front of the wing areas that hide waiting dancers from the audience. There are sometimes three or four teasers, creating different entrances from the wings to the stage. The choreographer will refer to them by number to let you know where you should be.

CHAPTER 4
THE BIG DAY

After the many hours of hard work and dedication you put into the rehearsal process, you will reach your reward: the recital. You have practiced the moves a thousand times and deserve to enjoy every leap, step, and turn. You are prepared for this moment—go onstage and have fun!

Arrival

When you arrive on the night of the recital, make sure a backstage volunteer knows you are present. Some teachers may give a special warm-up class before the performance. After the warm-up, keep your muscles warm by wearing layers of clothing over your costume.

It is important to practice good backstage behavior—especially the night of the show. Most likely, parent helpers will take your group into the wings at the appropriate time. This keeps the wing space quiet and clear. You must listen closely to the people in charge. The backstage rules may sometimes seem strict. However, they are an important part of putting on the show.

Warnings

As you are warming up and putting on your makeup and costume, you will hear the stage manager yell a series of time warnings. These warning calls usually begin about forty-five minutes before the curtain goes up. Someone will yell, "Forty-five minutes to curtain!" and excitement will begin to fill the air. There are then thirty-minute, fifteen-minute, ten-minute, and five-minute calls. The very last call is, "Places, please!" and every dancer will take his or

● Pay close attention to warning calls so you'll be in the right place at the right time.

her place, ready to perform. It is important to answer the stage manager's calls with a loud, "Thank you!" so that he or she knows you have heard each one.

Waiting in the Wings

When you hear the call, "Places, everyone!" you will probably feel a buzz of excitement run through the cast and crew. However difficult it may be, it is important to remain quiet backstage. Listen as the audience quiets down, waiting for the magic to begin.

As you stand in the wings before it is your turn to dance, you might be tempted to peek out to see the audience. The excitement might make it seem impossible to wait. Chances are, however, if you can see the audience, they can see you. Be a professional and stay out of sight. You'll have your chance—not only to see the audience, but also to thrill them once you are onstage.

Facing Your Fear

Many performers, not just dancers, deal with stage fright. This is an uneasy feeling of nervousness just before a performance. Your heart might beat fast, your palms might sweat, or you might even feel as if you cannot go onstage. Stage fright is very common and a completely normal response to the excitement of performing. After all of the hard work you put into preparing the show, it is natural to feel anxious before going out in front of an audience.

There are different ways to help ease stage fright. You may want to practice deep breathing. Take a few quiet moments alone before the performance to close your eyes and focus on taking full, deep breaths. Relax and visualize yourself doing every aspect of your performance perfectly. If you are having a hard time controlling your fear, ask another dancer or the choreographer how they would handle it. Try different methods to see what works for you. Remember that as you perform more, the stage will become more comfortable.

● Talking to a fellow dancer can help you deal with stage fright.

31

● Have fun with your performance. If you enjoy being onstage, the audience will enjoy watching you dance.

With experience, you may end up loving the stage, and find you are the *most* comfortable with an audience watching you.

Making Stage Fright Work for You

Some dancers have even found ways to use their stage fright. Since it is really just extra energy, these dancers have learned to use their fear to push themselves. If you feel anxious before a performance, try to harness that energy and use it to leap higher, dip lower, and spin faster. Make your fear your friend—you'll be surprised by how well you perform.

Being Onstage

Once you start dancing, your job as a performer has truly begun. There are two key things to remember while you perform. First, enjoy being onstage. Above all, you are there to experience the dance itself. Put your heart and soul into your performance and feel the pleasure of doing what you love.

Your second job as a performer is to allow the audience to experience the dance with you. If you feel the magic of the dance, the audience will feel it too. It is your time to shine—and share your talent.

Accidents Happen

No matter how prepared you are, onstage accidents can

happen. A dancer might trip and fall. A costume could be misplaced—or even get stuck on another dancer. A technical problem could cause the music to stop or the lights to change suddenly. Accidents like these happen to every dancer during his or her career. If anything should go wrong while you are performing, remember to be a professional. Unless you are hurt, keep dancing. The show must go on!

Your Bow

At the end of the show, you will come out to take your bow. A dancer's bow is his or her way of thanking the audience for coming to the show. Be gracious. The opportunity to perform is a well-deserved yet special gift. Use your bow to thank the people who supported you through the process, as well as everyone in the audience. They will, in turn, thank you with their applause. At some recitals, all of the classes will come onto the stage at the end of a show for a "finale," which is a group bow.

After the Show

After everyone has bowed and the curtain has come down, take the time to thank everyone for his or her dedication to the show. The crew, your teacher, the backstage volunteers, and the other dancers have all worked hard toward a great performance. Let your mind wander back through the process and you'll remember how each person played a part in making this night special. The show was magical because you all came together to make it a success.

Think back to your first day of dance class and how far you have come since then! Look forward to next year's performance and keep working toward your dreams.

● Take pride in your curtain call—it is your chance to thank the audience for coming to the show.

The Thrill of It All

From the first rehearsal to opening night, the process of putting a show together is an electrifying experience. Doing what you love with a team of dedicated people is both fulfilling and fun. When you feel ready, try it yourself. You'll be rewarded with the thrill of performing onstage. Break a leg!

Now that you have taken part in dance recitals, you may be ready to move on to bigger, more elaborate shows. As your appetite for performing grows, look into different productions that are going on around you. Many communities have amateur theater groups. Find out what shows are being put on and if there are ways for you to participate. Taking part in community performances is a great way to meet new people that share your passion for performing. You might even want to audition for large-scale shows in big cities. The more you experience, the more you will grow as a performer. Be proud of yourself as you see your dance skills improve. Don't hesitate to reach for the stars. With hard work and dedication, you'll surely soar!

"Dancers are passionate, hardwork-
ing, open, dedicated to their craft...we
are members of a very special breed."
—professional dancer, Julio Monge

GLOSSARY

choreography (kor-ee-**og**-ruh-fee) The art of creating and arranging dance movements.

cue (**kyoo**) The last words, line, or technical effect that immediately precedes a change in a performance; a stage signal.

downstage (**down**-stayj) The part of the stage near the audience.

duet (doo-**et**) A dance performed by two dancers.

finale (fuh-**nal**-ee) A final group bow for dancers at the end of a dance recital.

pas de deux (pa **di** du) A dance for two performers.

pas de quatre (pa di **ka**-truh) A dance for four performers.

responsibility (ri-spon-suh-**bil**-uh-tee) A duty or job.

solo (**soh**-loh) A dance for one performer.

souvenirs (soo-vuh-**nihrz**) Objects that you keep to remind you of a place, a person, or an event.

spacing (**spayss**-ing) Positioning dancers onstage for a performance to achieve the best overall look.

stage fright (**stayj frite**) A feeling of nervousness or fear experienced by performers prior to appearing before an audience.

technique (tek-**neek**) A method or way of doing something that requires skill.

upstage (**up**-stayj) The back part of the stage, farthest from the audience.

visualize (**vizh**-oo-uh-lize) To picture something in your mind.

volunteer (vol-uhn-**teer**) To offer to do a job, usually without pay.

wings (**wingz**) The areas to the right and left sides of a stage where performers wait before going onstage.

For More Information

Organization

Actors' Equity Association
165 West 46th Street, 15th Floor
New York, NY 10036
(212) 869-8530
Web site: http://www.actorsequity.org

Web Sites

Due to the changing nature of Internet links, the Rosen Publishing Group, Inc., has developed an online list of Web sites related to the subject of this book. This site is updated regularly. Please use this link to access the list:

http://www.rosenlinks.com/ccld/perform/

FOR FURTHER READING

Books

Hamilton, Linda H. *Advice for Dancers: Emotional Counsel and Practical Strategies*. San Francisco, CA: Jossey–Bass Publishers, 1998.

Jacob, Ellen. *Dancing: The All-in-One Guide for Dancers, Teachers and Parents*. New York: Variety Arts Books, 1999.

Magazines and Publications

Curtain Call Dance Club Revue
P.O. Box 709
York, PA 17405-0709
Web site: http://www.cckids.com

Dance
333 7th Avenue, 11th Floor
New York, NY 10001
(212) 979-4803
Web site: http://www.dancemagazine.com

Dancer
2829 Bird Avenue, Suite 5 PMB 231
Miami, FL 33133
(305) 460-3225
Web site: http://www.danceronline.com

Dance Spirit
Lifestyle Ventures, LLC
250 West 57th Street, Suite 420
New York, NY 10107
(212) 265-8890
Web site: http://www.dancespirit.com

BIBLIOGRAPHY

Bussell, Darcey and Patricia Linton. *The Young Dancer.*
New York: Dorling Kindersley Publishing, Inc., 1994.

"Choreography." Encyclopedia Britannica Online.
Retrieved May 2003 (subscription service)

Craine, Debra and Judith Mackrell. *The Oxford Dictionary of Dance.* New York: Oxford University Press, 2002.

"Dance." Encyclopedia Britannica Online. Retrieved May 2003 (subscription service)

"Makeup." Encyclopedia Britannica Online. Retrieved May 2003 (subscription service)

Minton, Sandra Cerny. *Choreography: A Basic Approach to Using Improvisation.* Champaign, IL: Human Kinetics Publishers, 1997.

Schanker, Harry H. and Katherine Anne Ommannery. *The Stage and the School.* New York: Glencoe McGraw-Hill, 1999.

"Stage Design." Encyclopedia Britannica Online. Retrieved May 2003 (subscription service)

"Stage Machinery." Encyclopedia Britannica Online. Retrieved May 2003 (subscription service)

INDEX

About the Author

Kristin Kessel has a Master of Arts in dance/dance education from New York University and an undergraduate degree in Theater from Wagner College. She has written for *Pointe* magazine and currently teaches dance in a high school performing arts program.

Editor: Shira Laskin **Book Design:** Christopher Logan and Erica Clendening

Developmental Editors: Nancy Allison, CMA, RME, and Susan Epstein